THE BILL OF RIGHTS

A **TRUE** BOOK

by

Patricia Ryon Quiri

Children's Press®
A Division of Grolier Publishing

New York   London   Hong Kong   Sydney
Danbury, Connecticut

Reading Consultant
Linda Cornwell
Learning Resource Consultant
Indiana Department
of Education

Author's Dedication:
For Ken Muir,
my Grand Rapids dad.
With love.

The Bill of Rights on display
at the National Archives in
Washington, D.C.

Visit Children's Press on the Internet at:
http://publishing.grolier.com

Library of Congress Cataloging-in-Publication Data

Quiri, Patricia Ryon.
  The Bill of Rights / by Patricia Ryon Quiri.
      p.   cm — (A true book)
  Includes bibliographical references and index.
  Summary: Chronicles how the Bill of Rights came to be, as well as the
freedoms it guarantees. Details each of the amendments and demon-
strates how some have affected contemporary life in the United States.
    ISBN 0-516-20661-3 (lib. bdg.)   0-516-26427-3 (pbk.)
    1. United States. Constitution. 1st-10th Amendments.—Juvenile litera-
ture. 2. Civil rights—United States—Juvenile literature. [1. United States.
Constitution. 1st-10th Amendments. 2. Constitutional amendments—
United States. 3. Civil rights.] I. Title. II. Series.
JC599.U5Q57 1998
323'.0973—dc21   97-50285
                                                                  CIP
                                                                  AC

Contents

The Constitutional Convention
in Philadelphia, 1787

New Country

In May 1787, many important men met in Philadelphia, Pennsylvania, to make a plan for a new government of the United States. The young nation had just won its independence from Great Britain in 1783. England no longer ruled. A new nation was born.

The leaders of the country realized that the federal, or national, government had to be stronger. As it was, the states were quite independent from one another, and each state had a separate government. Many times, states argued among themselves. Each state controlled its own trading with other countries. The leaders of the young country knew things had to change.

The Constitutional Convention

The group of men who met in Philadelphia to strengthen the federal government included such important people as James Madison, Edmund Randolph, William Paterson, Benjamin Franklin, and George Washington. There

James Madison (top left), William Paterson (top right), Edmund Randolph (bottom left), and George Washington (bottom right). Two of the delegates to the Constitutional Convention, Washington and Madison, later became U.S. presidents.

were fifty-five delegates. They planned to create an entirely new government for the United States. The ideas for the new government would be written down in a document called the Constitution.

During the meetings held to plan the Constitution, there was a lot of arguing. Some delegates threatened to leave. Thanks to James Madison, who eventually became the fourth president, we have a record of all that went on during the meetings from his detailed notes.

Ratifying the Constitution

After four long, hot months of secret work, the Constitution was ready. Now the delegates had to go back to their states and persuade the people to accept, or ratify, the Constitution. They decided that if nine of the thirteen states accepted the Constitution, it would become the law of the land.

THE

FEDERALIST:

A COLLECTION

OF

ESSAYS,

WRITTEN IN FAVOUR OF THE

NEW CONSTITUTION,

AS AGREED UPON BY THE FEDERAL CONVENTION,
SEPTEMBER 17, 1787.

IN TWO VOLUMES.

VOL. I.

NEW-YORK:

PRINTED AND SOLD BY J. AND A. McLEAN,
No. 41, HANOVER-SQUARE.
M,DCC,LXXXVIII.

This book, published by the Federalists in favor of the Constitution, helped convince the states to ratify it.

Some people were in favor of the Constitution. They were called Federalists. But some people didn't like the Constitution. They were called Anti-Federalists.

Many Anti-Federalists thought that people's individual rights needed to be protected. They said the Constitution needed a bill of rights to guarantee their individual freedoms. The Anti-Federalists refused to accept the

Constitution unless there was a bill of rights.

At first, James Madison did not think a bill of rights was necessary. He thought the state constitutions already protected the people's rights. However, many Anti-Federalists started speaking out against the Constitution. They wanted a statement in the Constitution that would protect the rights and free-doms of every American.

Newspaper cartoons try to convince Virginia and New York to say yes to the Constitution.

By June 21, 1788, nine states approved the Constitution, and it became official. The only states that rejected the Constitution were Virginia, New York, North Carolina, and Rhode Island. These states held back partly because there was no bill of rights in the Constitution. Virginia had included a bill of rights in its state constitution in 1776. In 1780, Massachusetts had decided upon a similar bill of rights for its state constitution. Virginia and Massachusetts, along with New York and North Carolina, insisted that a bill of rights be added to the federal Constitution before it became the law of the land. Madison still didn't think a bill of rights was necessary, but he promised others he would work on changing the Constitution, in order to include protection of individual rights.

The Bill of Rights

The House of Representatives worked on amendments (additions) to the Constitution. When the amendments went to the Senate, the Senate accepted all but one. Then the states voted on them. Out of twelve proposed amendments, the states ratified ten.

17

A copy of the Bill of Rights

These amendments became known as the Bill of Rights.

The first ten amendments to the Constitution deal with the following subjects:

Amendment 1— This amendment grants people freedom of religion, freedom of speech, and freedom of the press. Freedom of religion means that people are free to worship any way they please. The United States was the first country ever to make

A demonstration to help Cuban refugees

freedom of religion a right. Freedom of speech allows people to speak their mind whenever they want to. Freedom of the press allows people to publish their opinions about anything in newspapers or any other written communication. This freedom helps democracy work. It gives media such as newspapers the right to criticize the American government.

The Right to Assemble Peacefully

The Bill of Rights gives people the freedom to gather together in public to express their opinion. Usually, their purpose is to try to convince others. These schoolchildren are demonstrating in Washington, D.C., to save free school lunches.

In 1995, women marched to the White House to demand equal rights. Others have demonstrated to save our forests or to stop the use of nuclear weapons.

Although everyone may not agree with their point of view, these people have a right to look for supporters for their cause.

The First Amendment also gives people the right to gather together in a peaceful manner. It gives people the freedom to petition the government. That way, if people feel the government is being unfair, they can ask supporters to sign a paper, or petition, stating what it is they are unhappy about.

Amendment 2— This amendment states that people have the right to keep and

bear arms. The amendment gives people the right to own guns.

Amendment 3—This amendment states that the government cannot force citizens to let troops stay in their houses. Before the Revolutionary War, Britain forced people to house British soldiers.

Amendment 4—This amendment says that government officials cannot enter a home and search for things. They must have a warrant, or court order, to do so. Before the Revolutionary War, the British entered houses without permission to search for smuggled goods.

In 1986, Lieutenant Colonel Oliver North appeared before the House Foreign Affairs Committee, where he pleaded the Fifth Amendment.

Amendment 5—This amendment states that a person is considered innocent of a crime until he or she is proven guilty in a court of law. It also states that a person does not have to answer any question that might make that person seem guilty of a crime.

Amendment 6—This amendment guarantees that every person has the right to a speedy and public trial.

All people who are arrested have a right to a lawyer and a trial by jury.

The amendment protects people who are taken to court. It says they must have a lawyer and a jury who are fair.

Amendment 7—If a person is sued for a sum of money over twenty dollars, this amendment guarantees him or her a trial by jury.

Amendment 8—This amendment protects the rights of those who are arrested. It says that they do not have to pay large amounts of money to get out of jail while they are waiting for a trial. It also says that cruel and unusual punishment is unconstitutional, or against the Constitution.

Amendment 9—This amendment guarantees that people have other rights besides those listed in the Constitution and the Bill of Rights.

Amendment 10—This amendment gives states the

powers that are not listed as powers of the federal government in the Constitution.

It took more than two years for the Bill of Rights to be ratified state by state. Finally, by December 15, 1791, the necessary number of states had agreed. Other amendments were added later. This was the only time in the history of the United States that so many amendments were accepted at one time.

Freedom of Religion is for Everybody

Americans have the freedom to practice any religion they choose. Each year, Guyanese–Americans celebrate the Hindu Spring Festival of Pagwah (below). Other Americans follow the religion of Islam (opposite page, bottom). Still others practice Buddhism (opposite page, top).

How the Bill of Rights Works

The Bill of Rights has led to many new laws and court decisions that protect the freedom of individuals. However, sometimes it is hard to decide whether a person's freedom can be protected without harming others. For

Members of the Ku Klux Klan, a post-Civil War group who believe that whites are superior to all other Americans

example, freedom of speech is protected by the Bill of Rights. But when one person's speech tells lies about another person, the government may move to prevent it.

At times demonstrations can lead to violence.

The same goes for the right to gather peacefully. During the 1960s and 1970s, some political demonstrations

against unfair treatment of
African-Americans or against
the Vietnam War (1957–73)
led to fighting in public. So

the courts made decisions about where, when, and how demonstrations could occur in public places. They based their decisions on whether or not the demonstrations would cause danger to others. They did not want the freedom of some people to interfere with the safety of others.

Other problems concern the right to privacy. When the police want information on a suspected criminal, they try to

Use of a wiretapping machine by the police is not always allowed under the law.

get it using many methods. The court has tried to decide whether or not the police can wiretap people's conversations and use it against them. To "wiretap" is to listen to a conversation secretly by means of an electronic device. In some cases, the court allows this. But in other cases, wiretapping cannot be used as evidence in court. The same goes for secret video-taping or filming.

The Bill of Rights makes it possible for every American to enjoy certain freedoms. But these freedoms must be interpreted and enforced by courts and lawmakers.

Ever since the Bill of Rights was written, different people have found different ways to interpret it. As times change, the way courts and lawmakers react to the Bill of Rights changes also.

The Founding Fathers who wrote the Constitution and the Bill of Rights laid the foundation for a free society. It was up to those who came afterward to make that society work.

To Find Out More

Here are some additional resources to help you learn more about the Constitution and The Bill of Rights:

 **Books**

The Constitution of the United States. The Bicentennial Keepsake Edition. Bantam Books, 1987.

Fritz, Jean. **Shh! We're Writing the Constitution.** G. P. Putnam's Sons, 1987.

Morris, Richard. **The Constitution.** Lerner Publications, 1985.

Morris, Richard. **The Framing of the Constitution.** U.S. Department of the Interior, 1986.

Quiri, Patricia Ryon. **The Constitution.** Children's Press, 1998.

Quiri, Patricia Ryon. **The Congress.** Children's Press, 1998.

Benjamin Franklin National Memorial

Franklin Institute Science Museum
222 North 20th Street
Philadelphia, PA 19103-1194
http://www.fi.edu/franklin/ rotten.html

Place to see a statue of Ben Franklin, as well as many of his original possessions

The Bill of Rights

http://www.legislate.com/ d/drights/htm

The complete text of the original document

Constitutional Rights Foundation

601 Kingsley Drive
Los Angeles, CA 90005

Helps young people better understand the values of the Constitution and the Bill of Rights

Independence Hall Association

Carpenters' Hall
320 Chestnut Street
Philadelphia, PA 19106
http://www.iha@libertynet.org

The guiding light behind "America's Most Historic Square Mile"

National Archives

700 Pennsylvania Ave. NW
Washington, DC 20408

The orginal document of the Bill of Rights is on display.

National Museum of American History

http://www.si.edu/ organiza/museums/nmah

Enter the Hands on History room to experience what life in the United States was like 200 years ago.

Important Words

amendment change

Anti-Federalists people who were against the Constitution

Constitution written plan for a national government

delegates representatives

Federalists people who were in favor of the Constitution

petition written document that calls for a change

ratify accept

unconstitutional against the ideas of the Constitution

warrant written order

wiretap listen to a conversation secretly by electronic means

Index

Meet the Author

Patricia Ryon Quiri lives in Palm Harbor, Florida, with her husband Bob and their three sons. Ms. Quiri has a B.A. in elementary education from Alfred University, located in upstate New York. She currently teaches second grade in the Pinellas County School system. Other books by Ms. Quiri include *The Constitution, The Presidency, The Supreme Court, The Declaration of Independence,* and *The Congress.* Ms. Quiri has also written a five-book series on American landmarks and symbols, as well as many other books for Children's Press.